Angry Swearing Cats

{·Swear Word Adult Coloring Book·}

Download free coloring pages at
www.swearandrelax.com

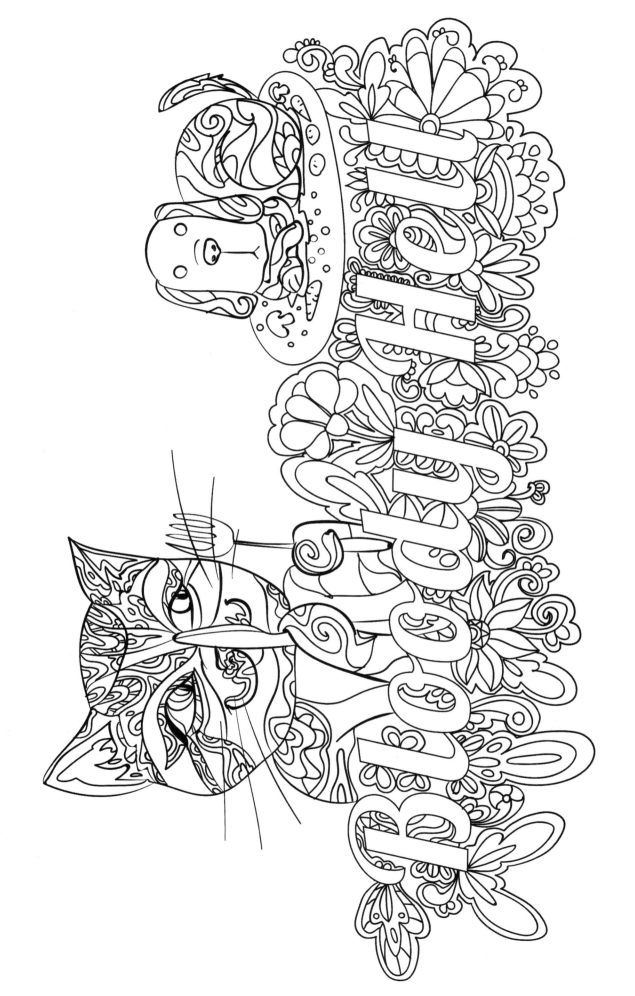

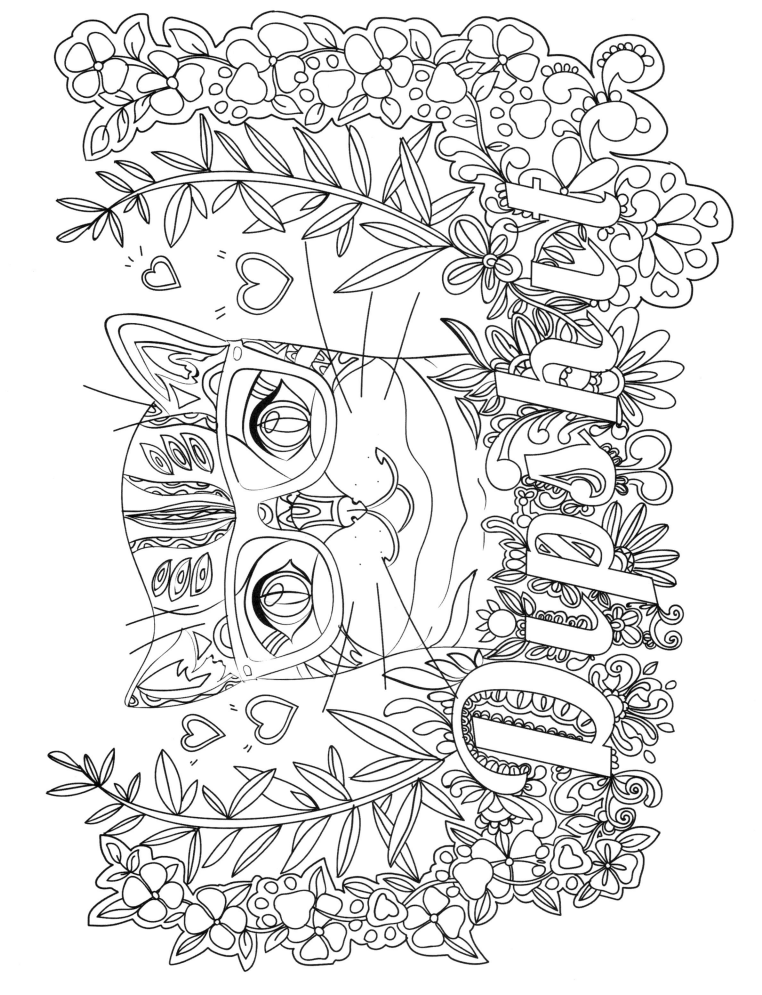

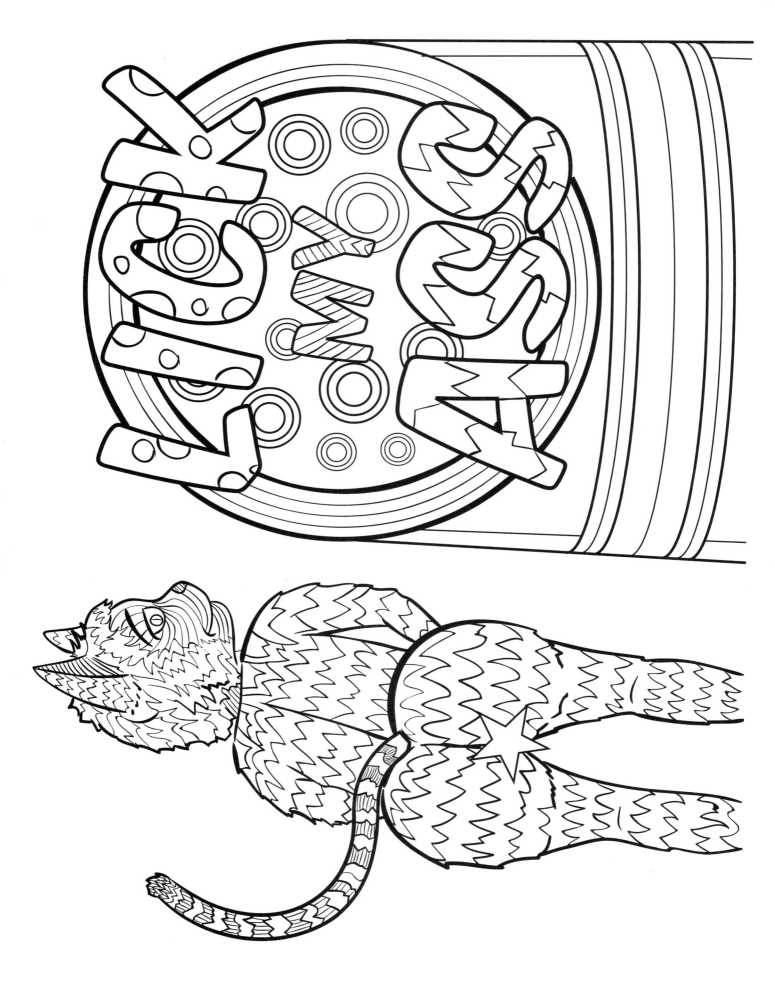

FREE SAMPLES

Download free coloring pages at
www.swearandrelax.com

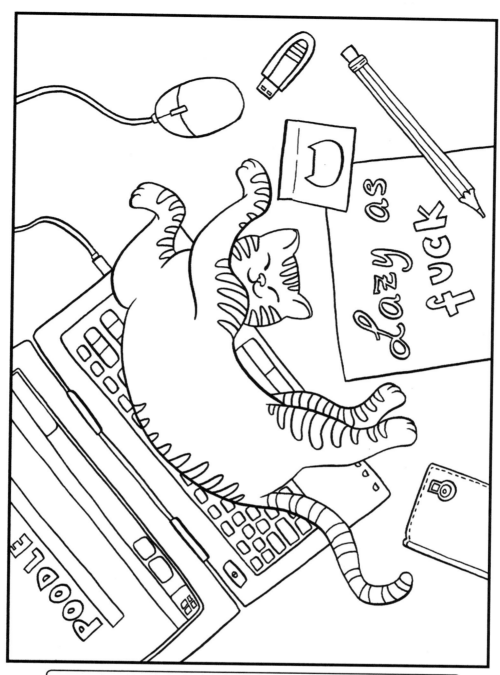

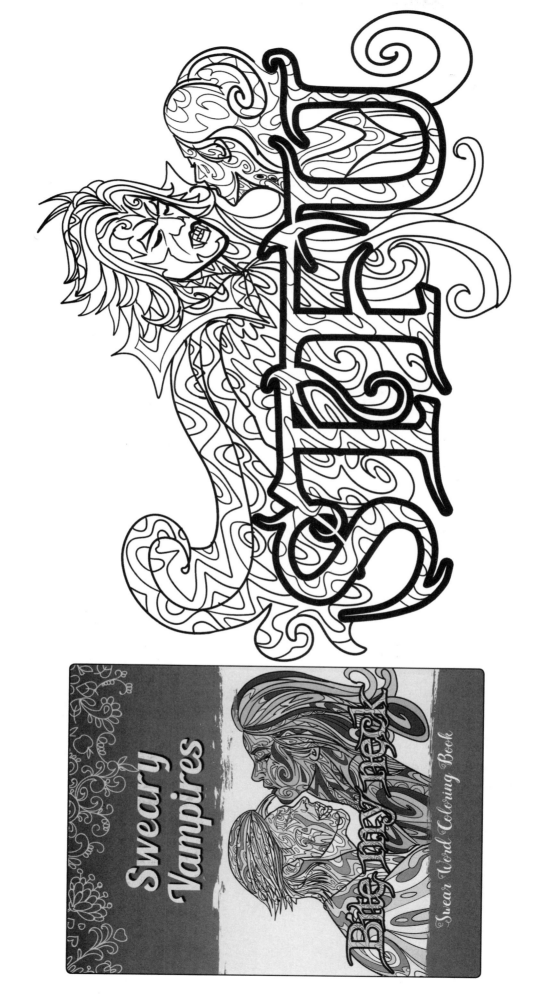

STOP EATING THIS SHIT

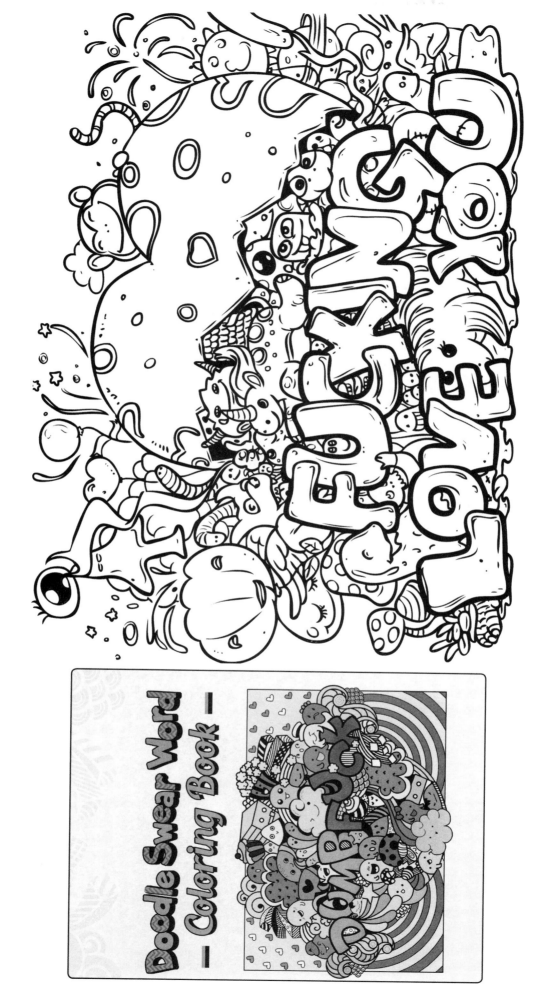

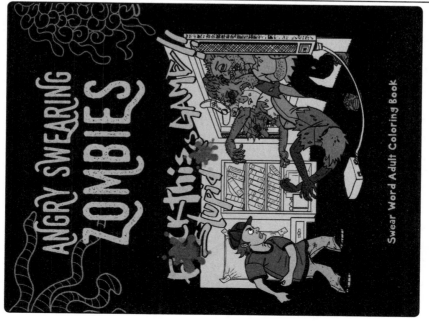

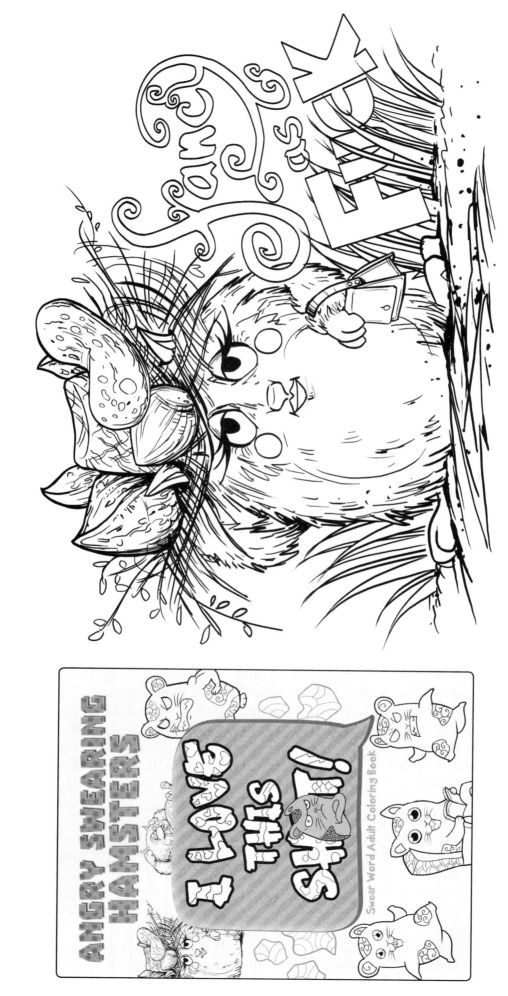

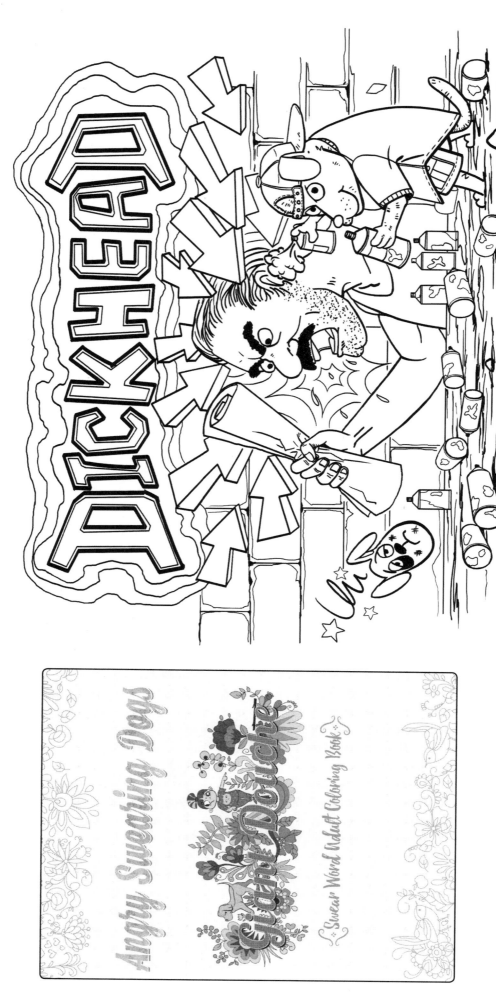